# BEE
# COLORING BOOK

## CRYSTAL
## COLORING BOOKS


ISBN-13: 978-1974063840
ISBN-10: 1974063844

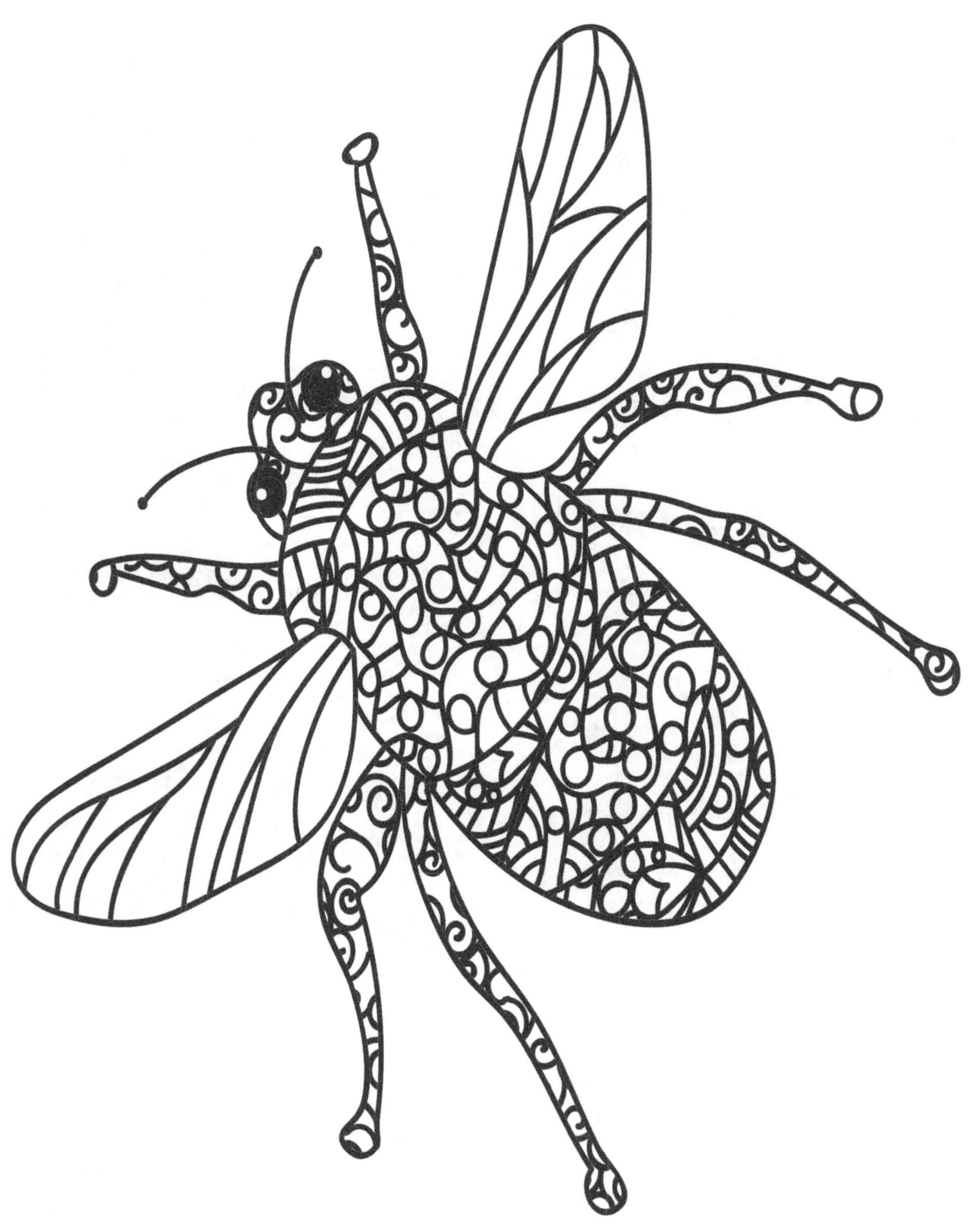

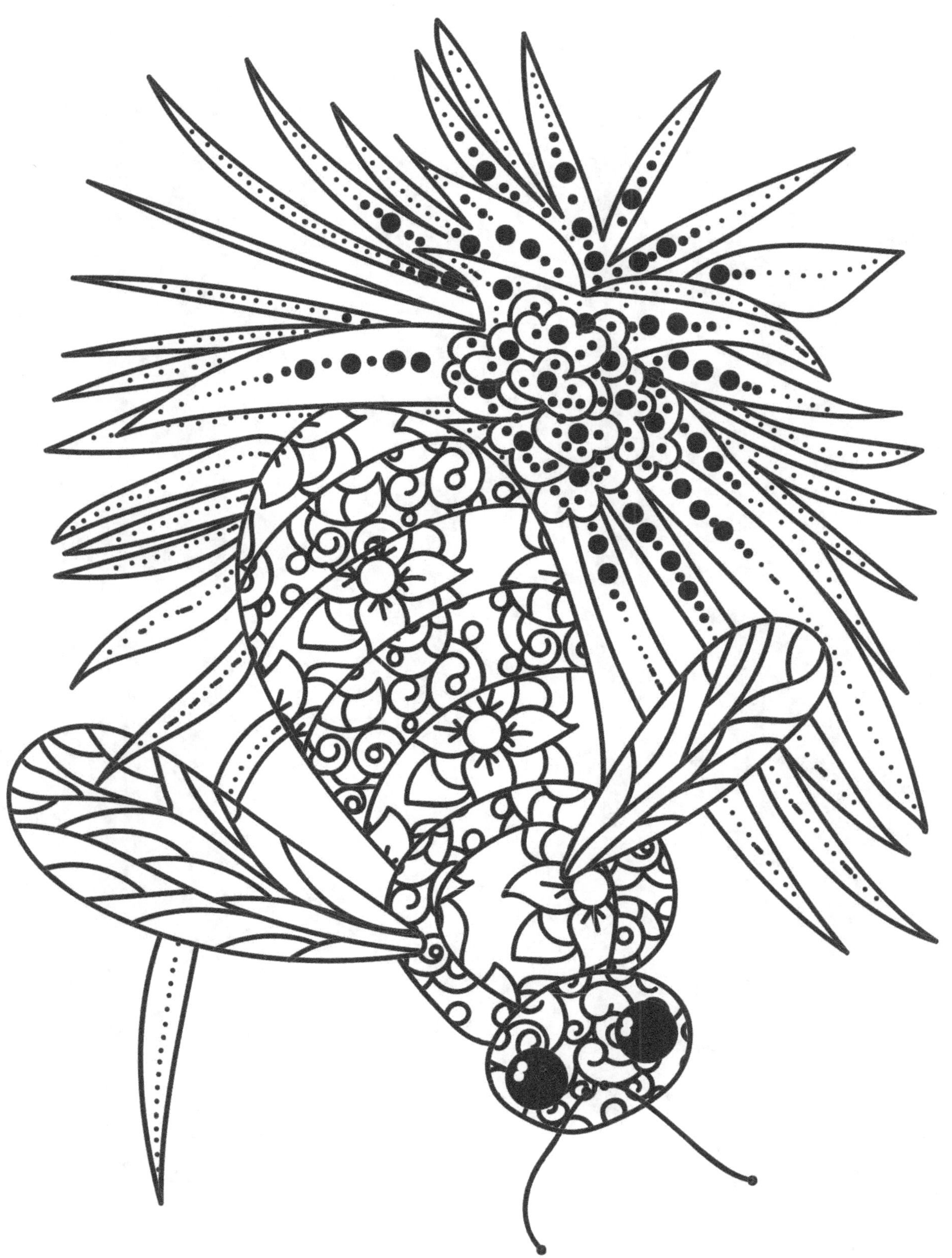

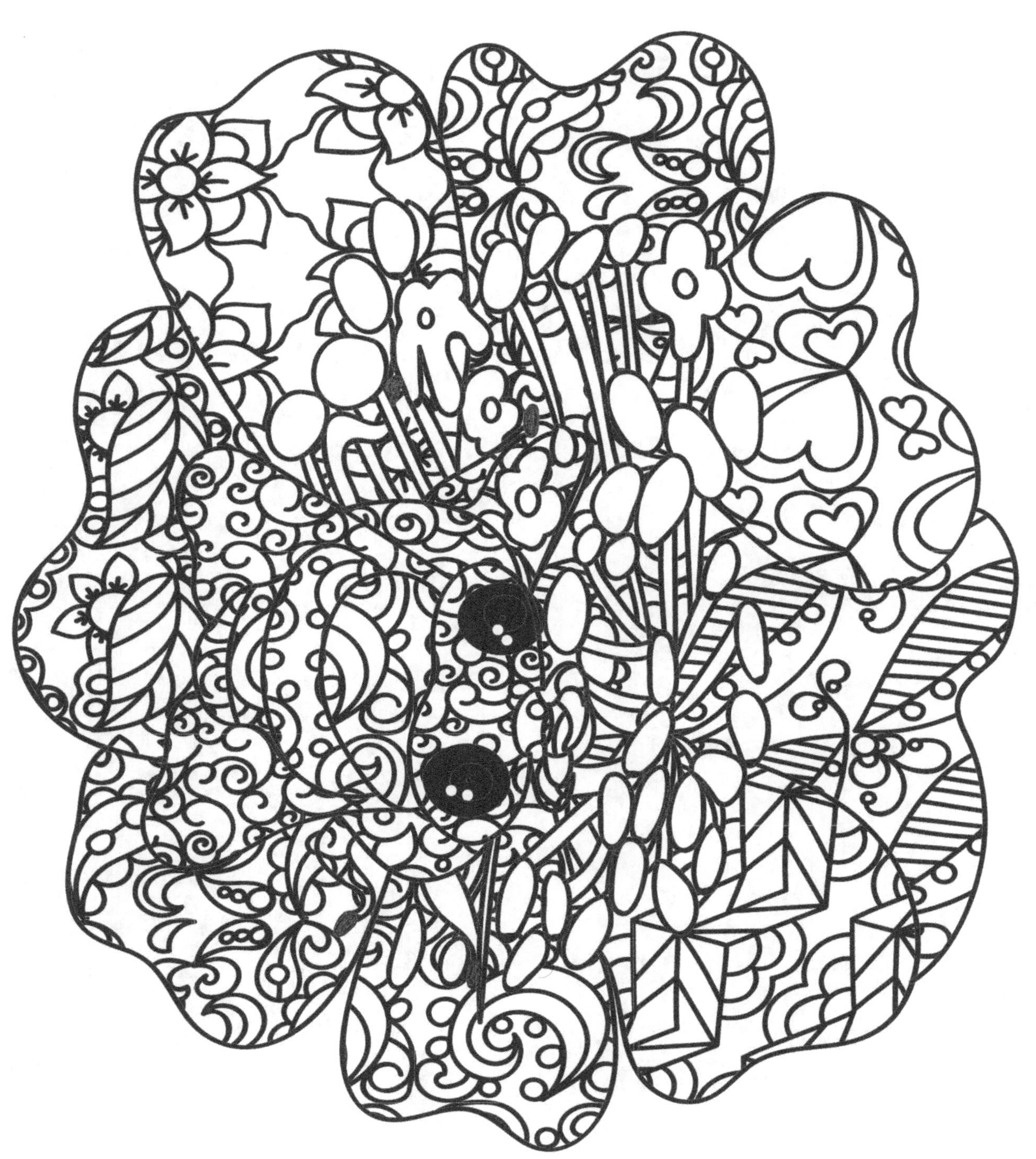

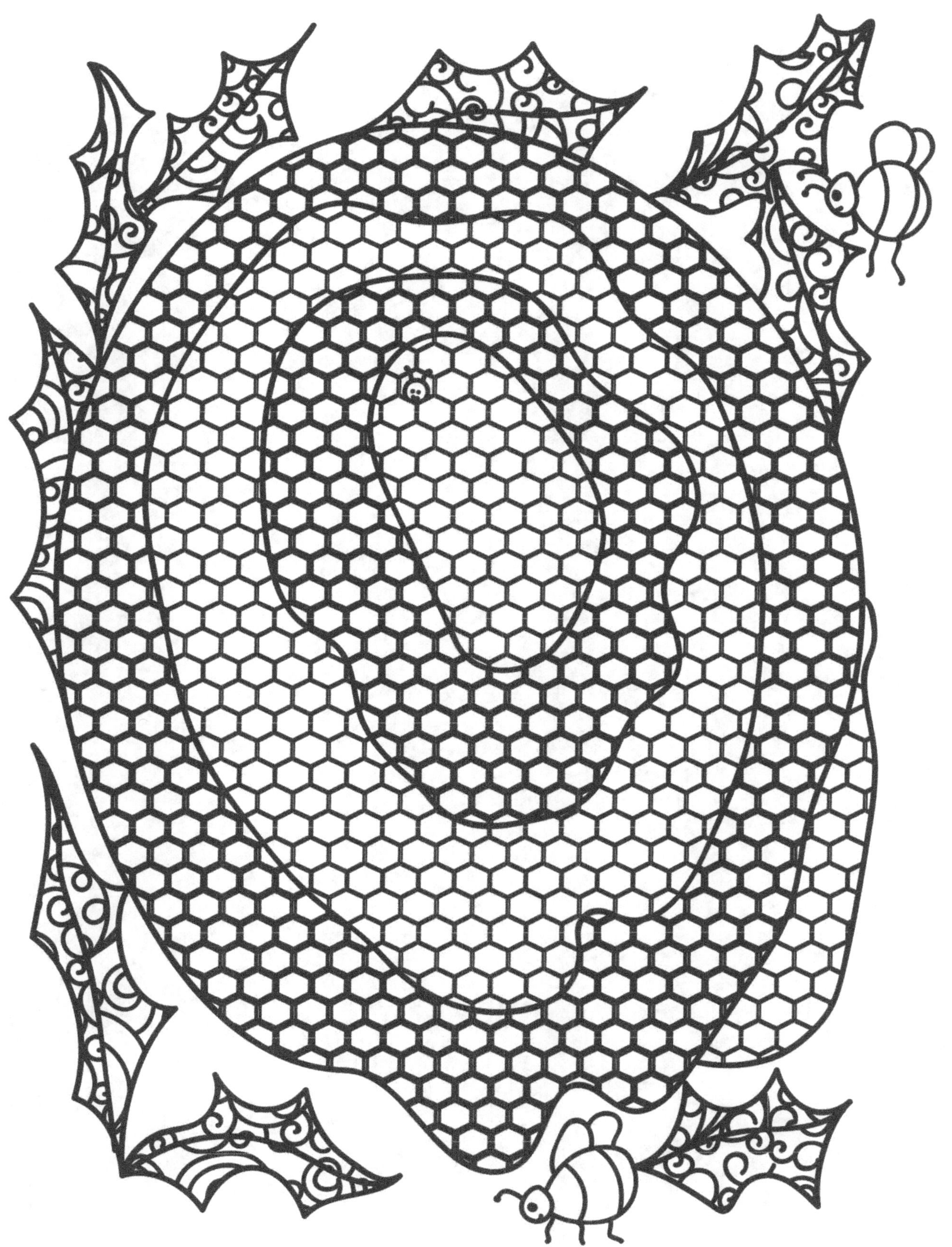

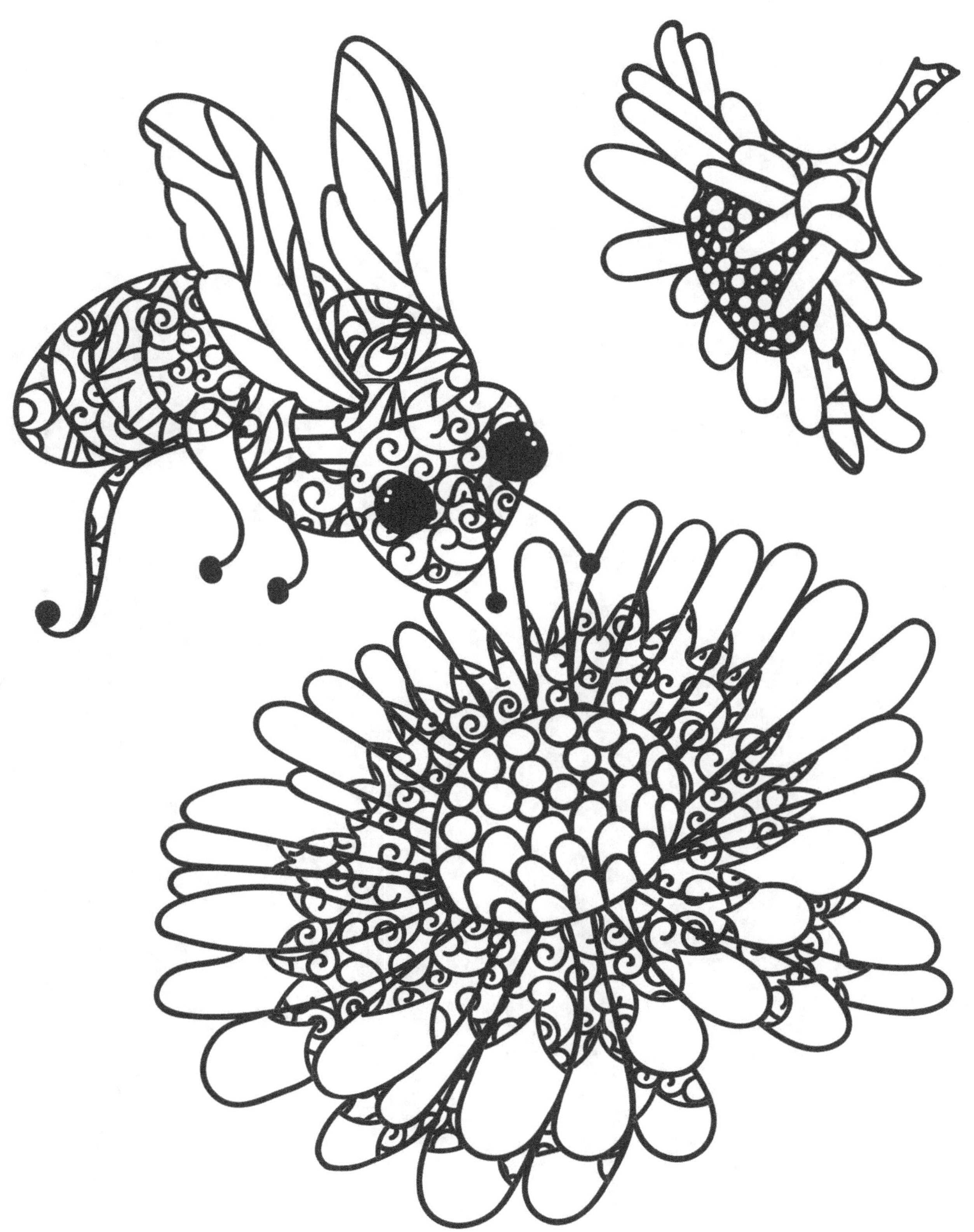

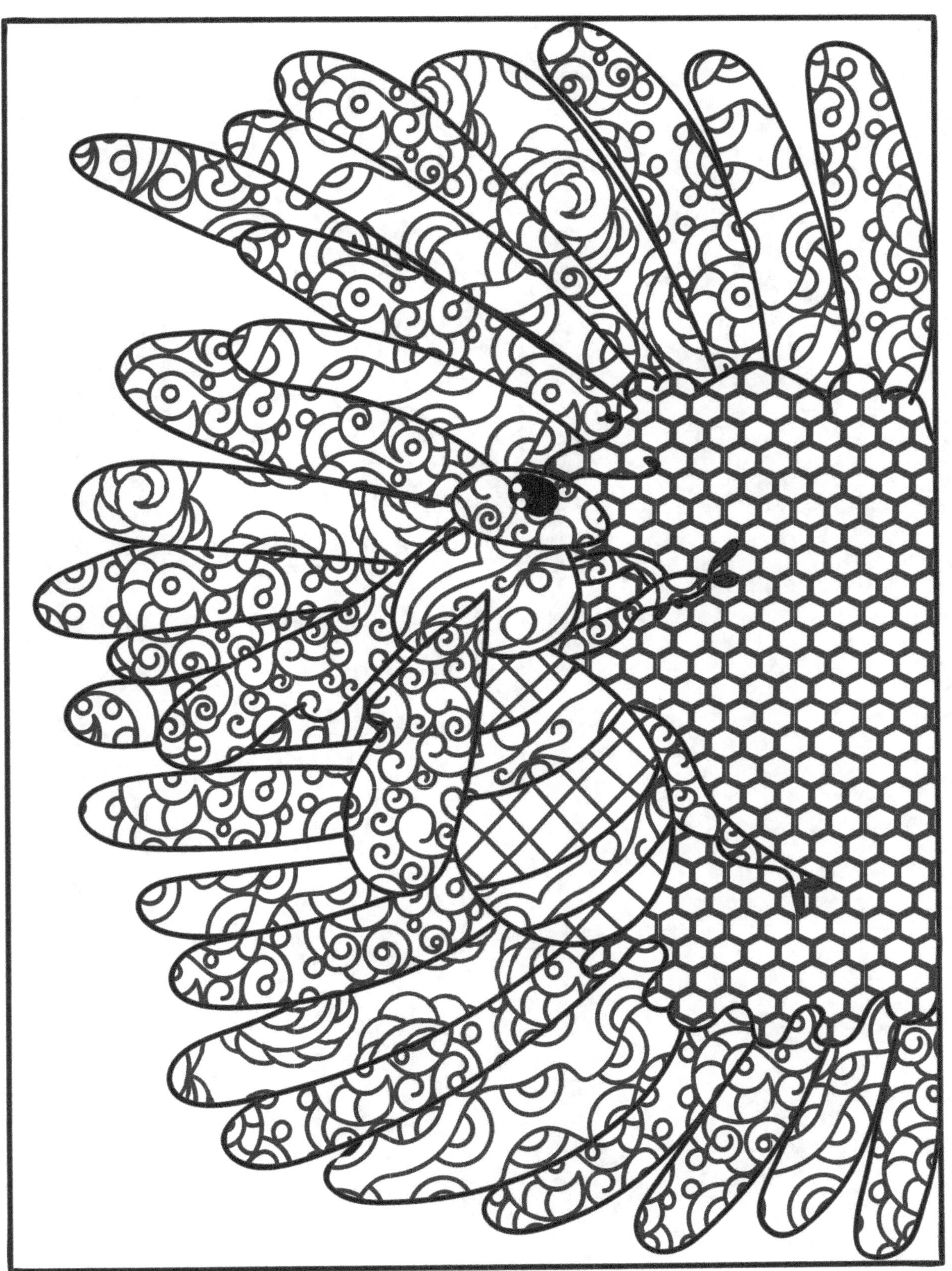

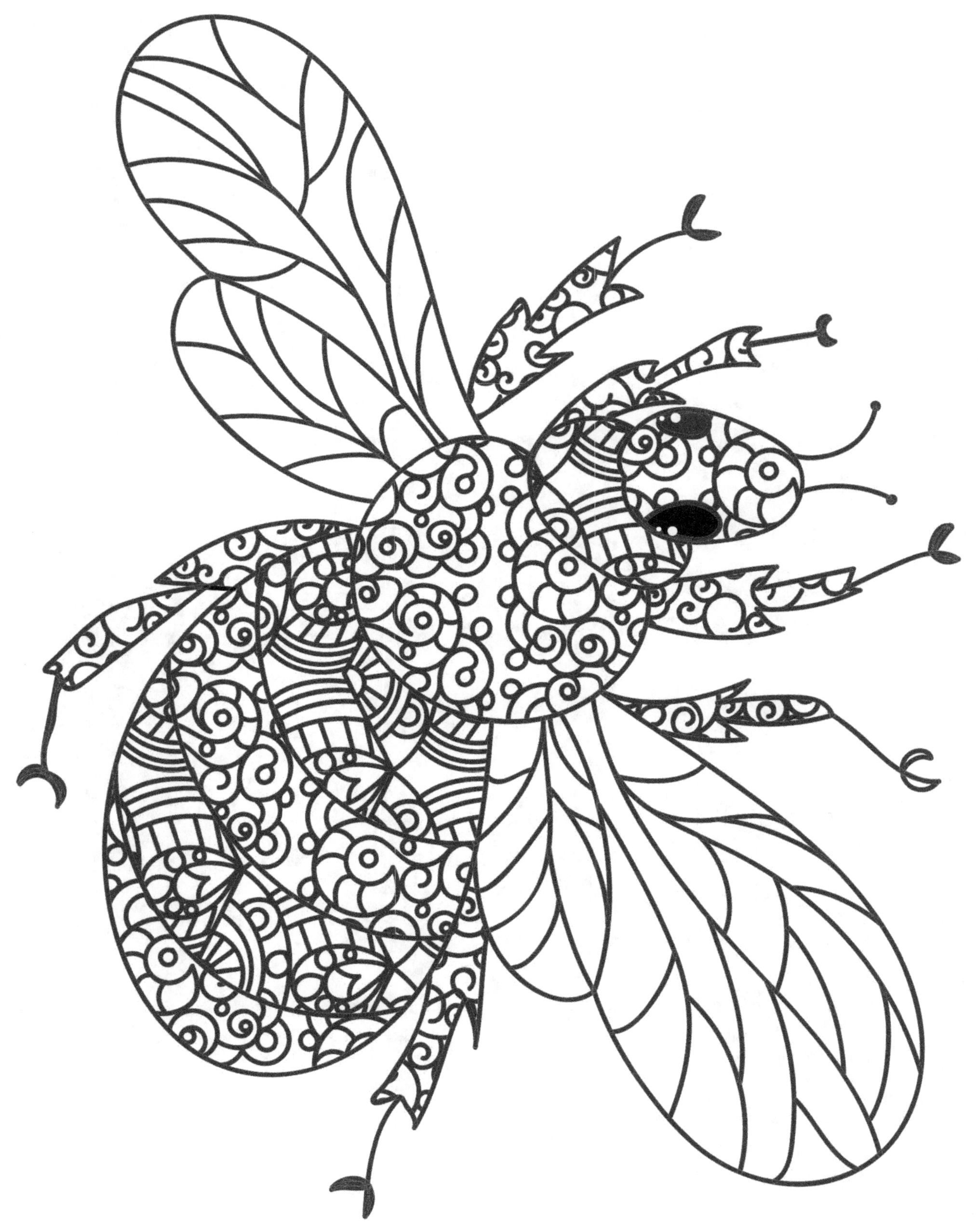

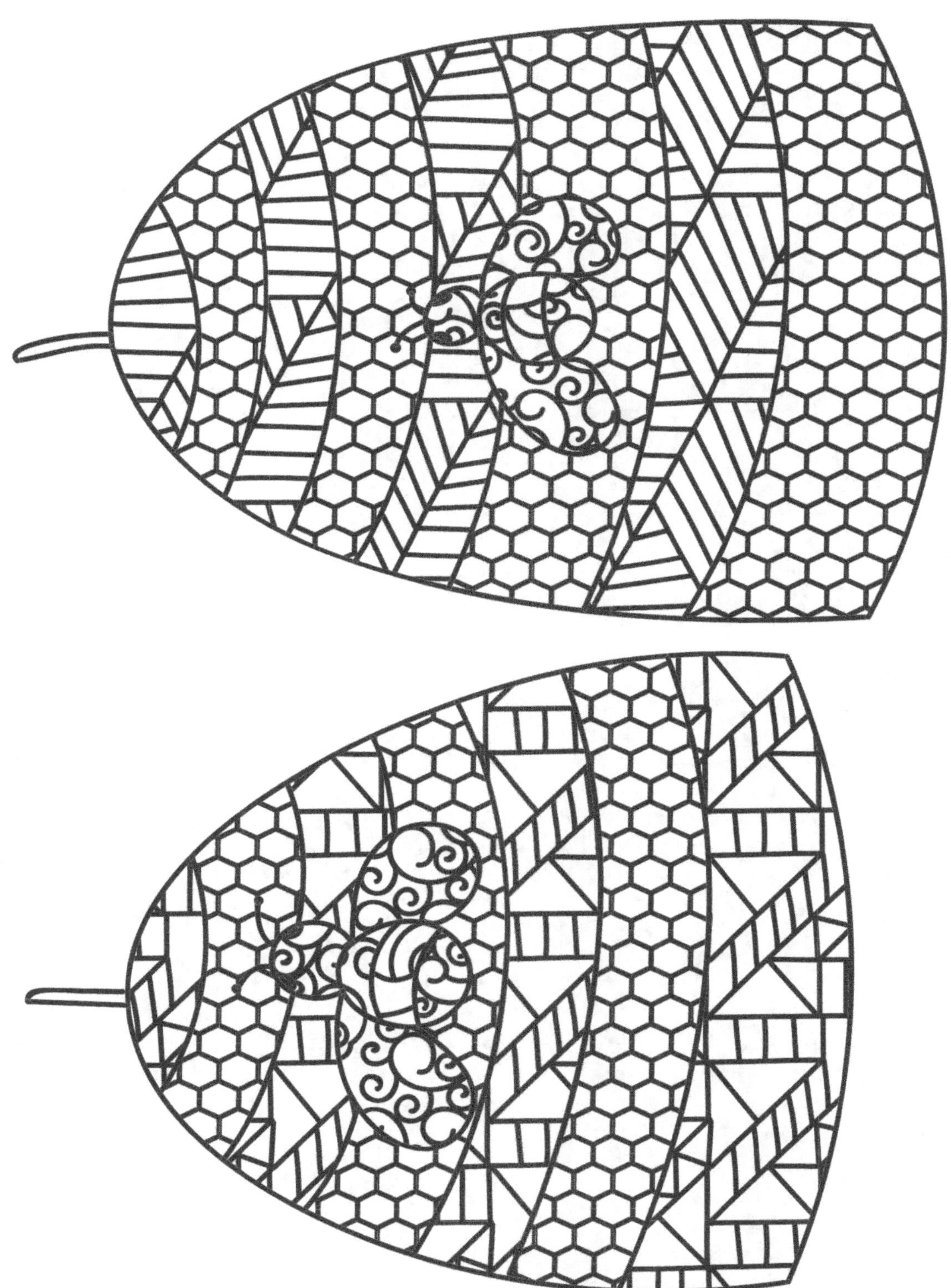

# COLOR TEST PAGE

# COLOR TEST PAGE